Alternative Energy

SOLAR POWER

Louise Kay Stewart

WAYLAND

First published in Great Britain in 2023 by Hodder & Stoughton

Editor: Elise Short
Design: Paul Cherrill
Illustration: DGPH Studio

The text in this book was previously published
in the series *Let's Discuss Energy Resources* and has been updated.

HB ISBN: 978 1 5263 2525 9
PB ISBN: 978 1 5263 2526 6

Printed and bound in China

FSC
www.fsc.org
MIX
Paper from
responsible sources
FSC® C104740

Wayland, an imprint of
Hachette Children's Group
Part of Hodder & Stoughton
Carmelite House
50 Victoria Embankment
London EC4Y 0DZ

An Hachette UK Company
www.hachette.co.uk
www.hachettechildrens.co.uk

CONTENTS

SOLAR POWER AS AN ENERGY RESOURCE

We use energy resources every day, without thinking about it! Cars burn fuel in engines to release the energy that turns their wheels. Sun shining through greenhouse windows warms the air to help plants grow. Most of the machines we use run on electricity made using energy resources.

Fossil fuel power

Almost two-thirds of the electricity used around the world today is generated using the energy created from burning fossil fuels, such as coal and gas. But burning these fuels releases gases that cause air pollution and greenhouse gases like carbon dioxide, which trap heat in the atmosphere, causing climate change. Fossil fuels are also non-renewable, which means they are running out.

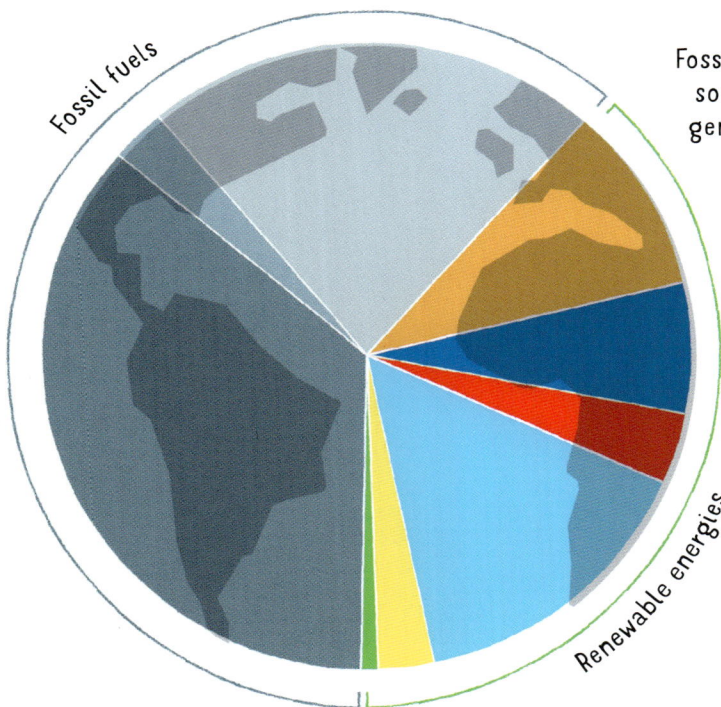

Fossil fuels

Renewable energies

Fossil fuels are the main sources of energy for generating electricity.

Fossil fuels	Renewable energies	
Gas 22.9%	Nuclear 9.8%	Hydro-electric 15%
Oil 2.5%	Wind 6.5%	Other renewables 2.7%
Coal 36%	Solar 3.6%	Other 0.9%

The major problem with using fossil fuels to generate electricity is the production of greenhouse gases that build up in the atmosphere.

Renewable energy resources

Renewable energy resources will not run out because they are in endless supply. These resources include wind, waves and tides. Using renewable energy for power produces far fewer greenhouse gases and less pollution than fossil fuels, so they aren't as harmful to our planet. Using energy from the Sun to make electricity is called solar power.

In this solar power farm, hundreds of panels capture solar energy and turn it into electricity.

HOW WE USE THE SUN'S ENERGY

The Sun is millions of kilometres away from Earth, but it is still our nearest star. Like other stars, the Sun is an enormous ball of incredibly hot gases. Solar energy from the Sun's gases moves through space to Earth in the form of heat and light radiation. We can use the energy in the Sun's radiation in different ways.

The Sun gives off huge amounts of light and heat, known as solar energy.

Solar collectors

Solar collectors on house roofs are used to heat water. These large glass panels contain dark pipes with liquid inside. The pipes absorb heat radiation from the Sun and warm the liquid. They carry the hot liquid inside the house to heat tanks of water.

Solar cells

Solar cells use the energy in the Sun's light rather than its heat to make power. Solar cells are devices that change sunlight directly into electricity in one step.

Solar heating

The simplest way in which we use the Sun's heat is to warm our homes. Glass windows that face the Sun let in heat radiation to warm the air that is trapped inside.

Solar power stations

We can also use the Sun's energy to make electricity. In a solar power station (see pages 8–9), the Sun's heat is used to make electricity. Devices called solar furnaces turn solar heat energy into electricity.

SOLAR POWER STATIONS

In a solar power station, devices called solar furnaces use the Sun's heat to make electricity. Even on the hottest summer's day, sunlight on a puddle of water only makes it warm. Solar power stations need a way of concentrating heat from the Sun to use it to make electricity.

Mirrors and receivers

Solar power station furnaces have systems of mirrors to reflect, or bounce, sunlight that falls over a large area. The mirrors focus, or concentrate, it into a receiver. This makes the receiver heat up to incredibly high temperatures of up to 2,000°C.

From heat to electricity

Solar power stations and fossil-fuelled power stations work in a similar way. Both use heat to produce steam. The steam drives machines that make electricity. In a solar power station, instead of burning coal or gas to make heat, heat from the Sun is used.

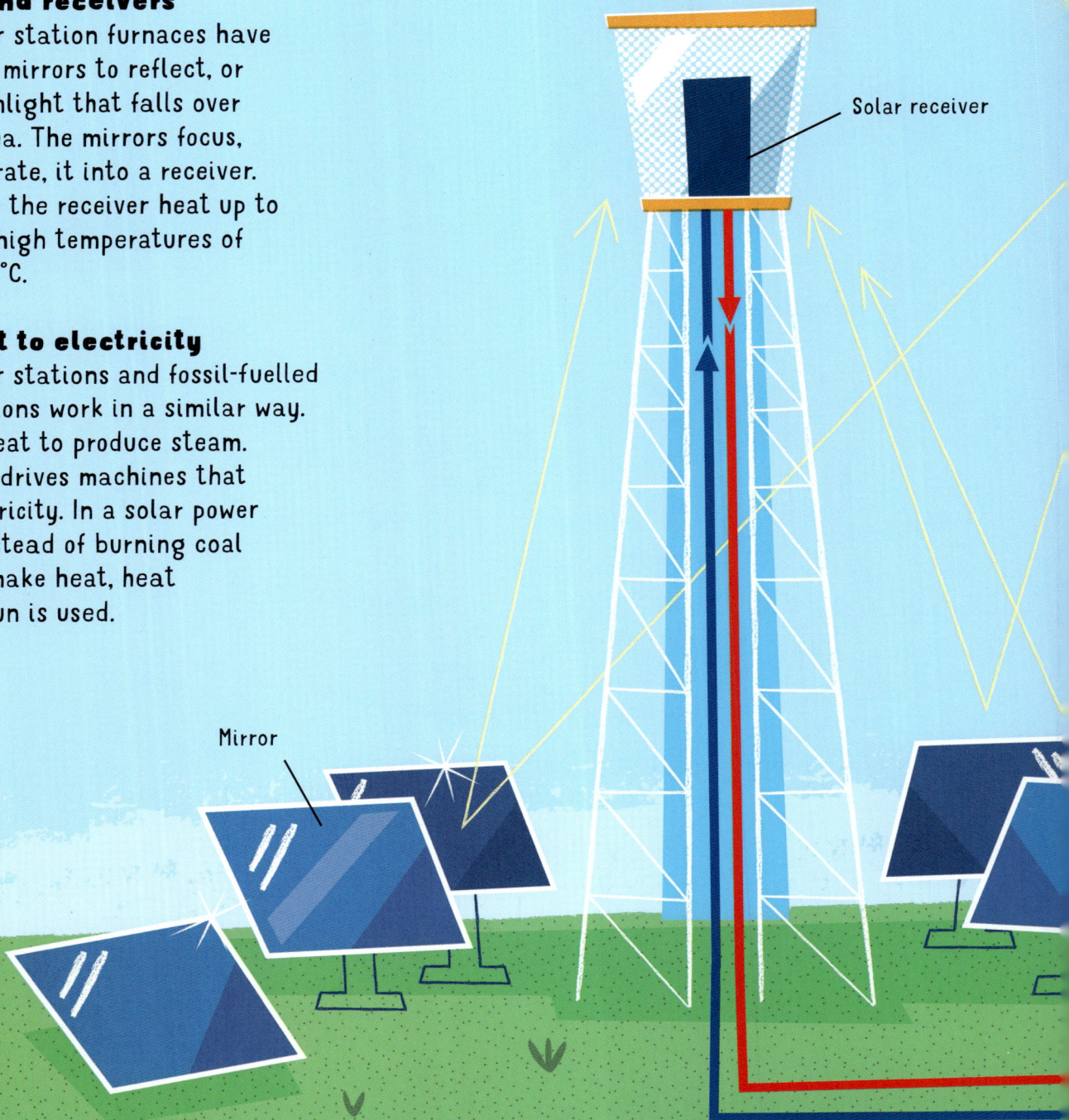

Solar receiver

Mirror

Turbines and generators

In a power station, heat is used to boil water to make the steam. The moving steam spins the blades of a turbine, which looks a bit like a propeller. A machine called a generator then converts that movement energy into electrical energy.

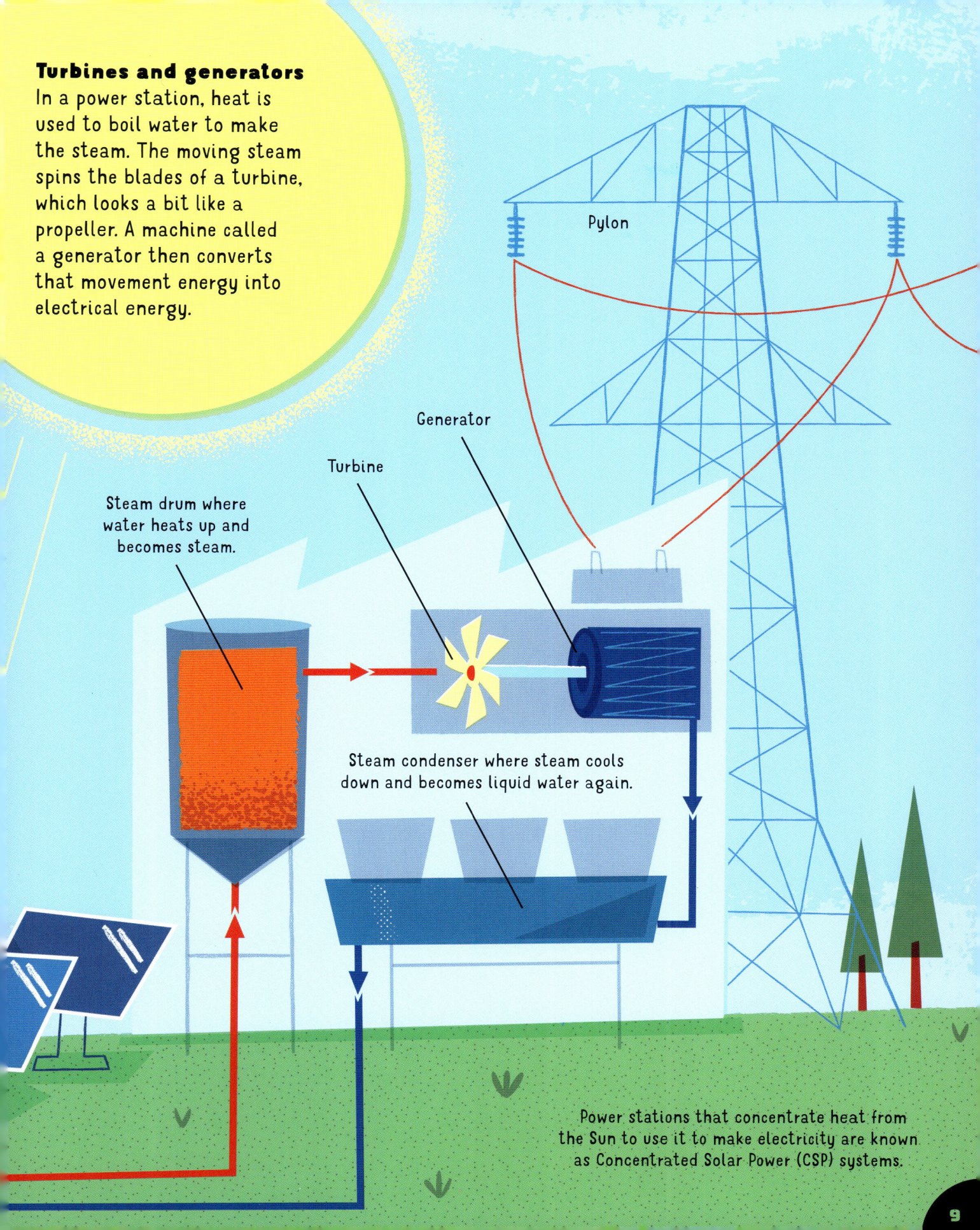

Pylon

Generator

Turbine

Steam drum where water heats up and becomes steam.

Steam condenser where steam cools down and becomes liquid water again.

Power stations that concentrate heat from the Sun to use it to make electricity are known as Concentrated Solar Power (CSP) systems.

HOW SOLAR CELLS WORK

Solar cells turn light energy from the Sun into electricity.
Solar cells are also known as photovoltaic, or PV, cells.

PV cells

A solar, or PV, cell is made up of special materials that are sandwiched together in layers. The layers work together to convert light energy from the Sun into electricity. Many solar cells are wired together to form solar panels.

A solar (PV) cell

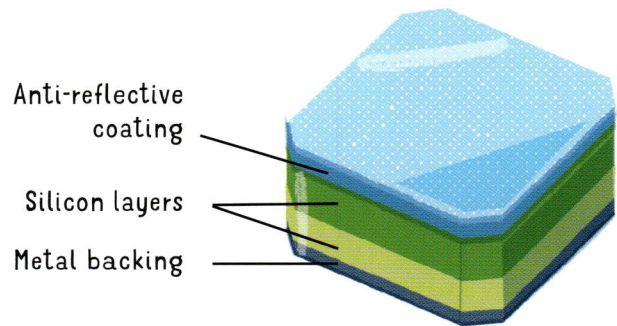

Anti-reflective coating

Silicon layers

Metal backing

Glass or plastic on top of the cell protects the silicon inside. It also has a coating to stop useful light reflecting away from the cell.

Light energy to electricity

Most solar cells contain two very thin layers of silicon. Silicon is a material that can be extracted from sand. The silicon in each layer is coated with a different chemical. When light energy hits the silicon layers, it makes a very small electric current start to flow between them.

From cells to wires

Metal strips on top of the cell conduct, or carry away, the electricity from the silicon layers to wires. The wires take the electricity to where it is needed. Individual solar cells are connected together in solar panels to provide more power.

A single solar cell makes only a little electricity. Groups of solar cells can provide electricity for whole buildings.

The technology used to generate electricity from sunlight is known as a PV system.

HOW SOLAR POWER VARIES

Solar power can only be harnessed in the daytime and not at night. The amount of solar power available also varies between different parts of the world.

Sun and climate

Solar energy works best in areas with high amounts of sunlight and low cloud cover. Tropical climates are hot and sunny almost all year round. Climates like those in Europe and most of North America have sunny summers followed by cloudy winters with fewer hours of sunlight. Solar panels can work there in winter, but these areas could not have solar power as the only source of energy.

Solar energy received at Earth's surface

Lowest ▮▮▮▮▮ Highest

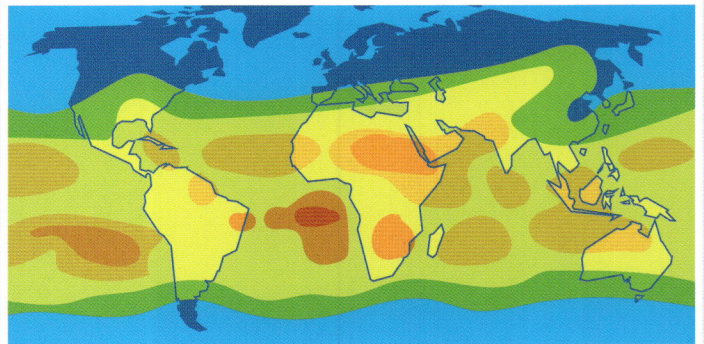

The greatest solar energy is generally received near the Equator and away from the poles.

Solar cells don't need direct sunlight to work and can even work on cloudy days. However, the stronger the sunshine, the more electricity is generated.

Storing solar

There are ways of storing solar energy to use during hours of darkness. PV systems can store the energy in rechargeable batteries. Solar power can only be stored for fairly short periods of time. It is mainly stored to be used overnight.

Power station storage

In solar power stations, energy may be stored as heat. Melted salts are heated in towers and then kept in tanks that prevent them losing heat. The energy may be used directly for heating and cooling, or it can be used to generate electricity.

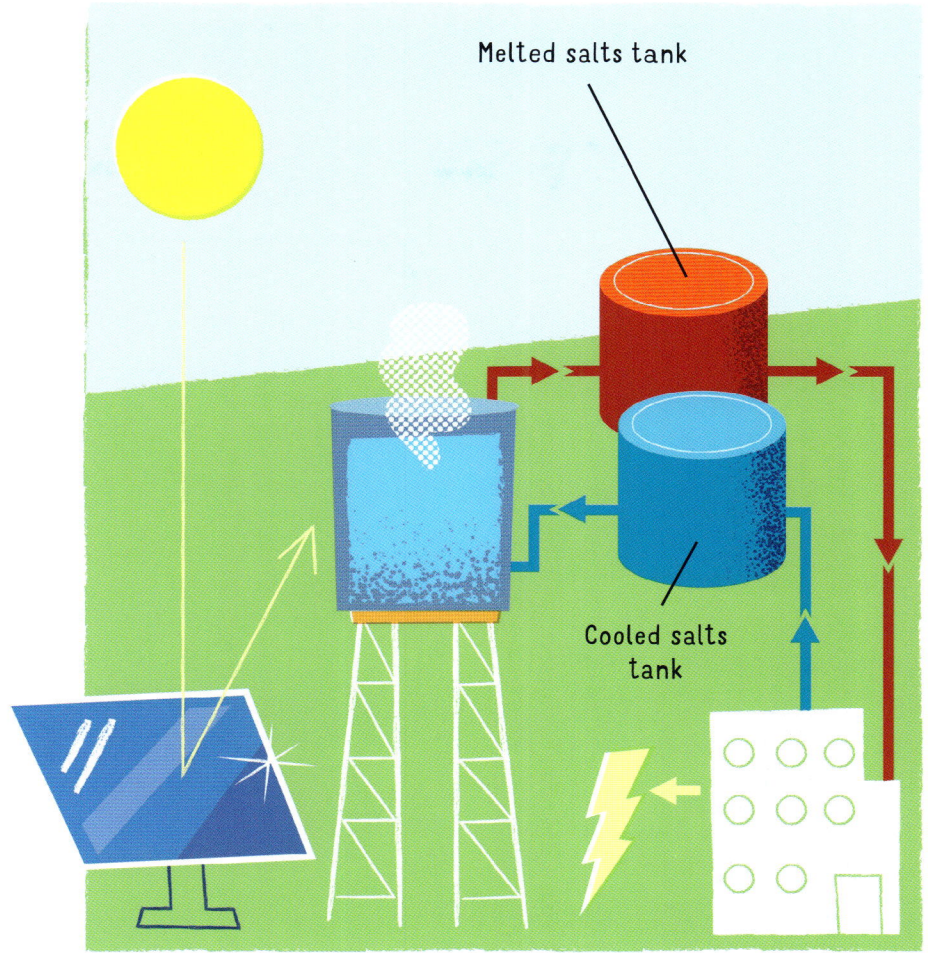

Melted salts tank

Cooled salts tank

This solar power station has salt tanks to store energy.

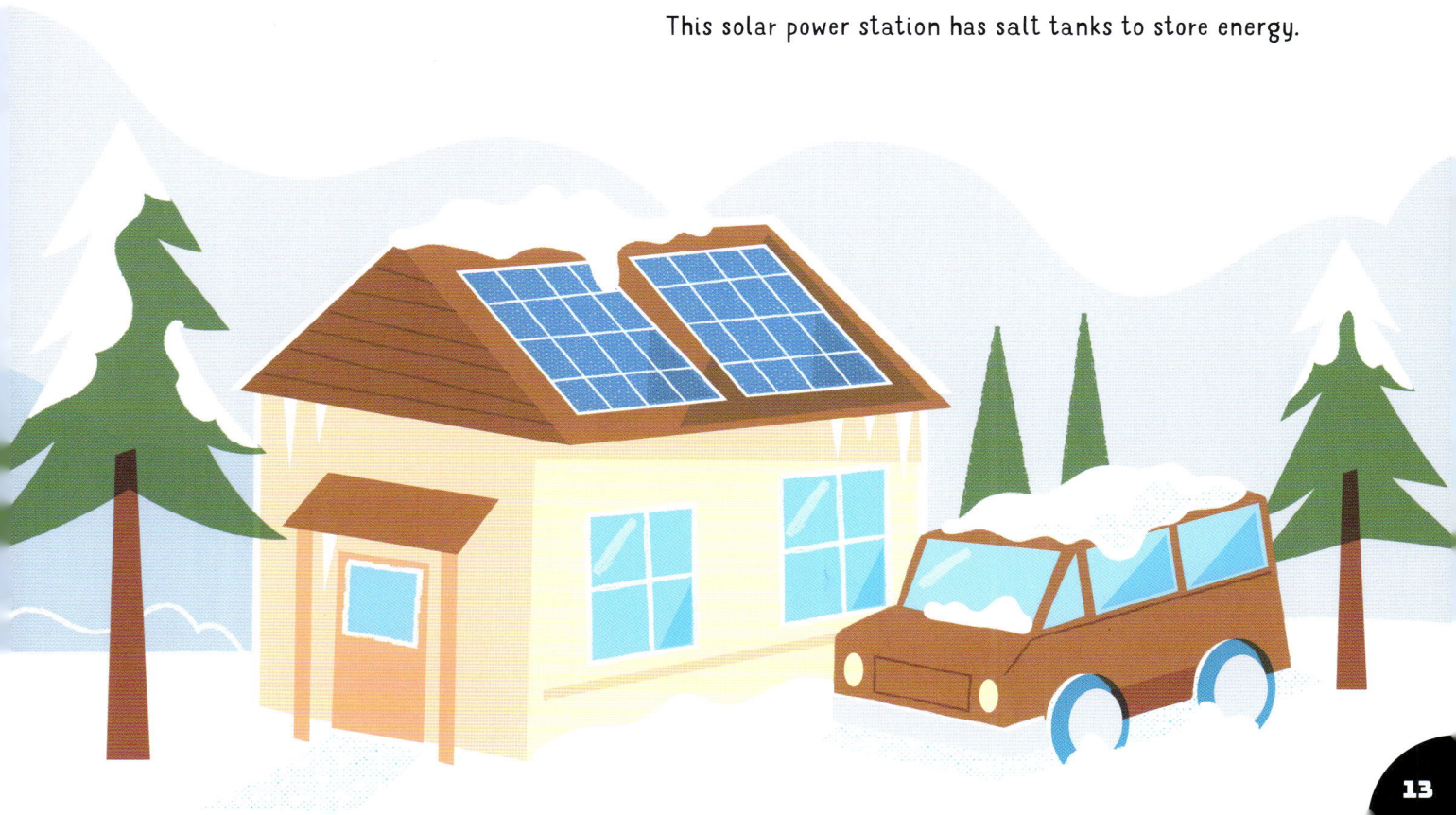

SOLAR CELLS FOR DIFFERENT NEEDS

One of the big advantages of solar power is that it can be generated where it is needed. PV cells and panels can be installed on anything from a calculator to a space station! They can be used by families, small communities and businesses to generate enough electricity for their own needs.

Remote places

Millions of people around the world do not have mains electricity because they live in remote places that are not connected to a power grid. Solar panels are being introduced in many remote places in sunny countries across the world, from African villages to farms in Australia. Solar radios, computers, lights, pumps and road signs are some of the many devices generating their own electricity, known as microgenerating, that have a massive impact in remote places.

Solar power brings electricity to remote places.

Built-in power

Solar panels are erected close to or on the structures that will use the electricity they produce. They can be fixed to the roofs of buildings or on the ground near a building. That way, there is no need for long cables to take the electricity to the people who use it.

Solar solutions

Solar panels are often angled so they face the Sun. Being angled also means rain and any dirt run off their surface. Modern buildings sometimes use special solar building materials instead of panels. These include roof tiles and window glass with built-in solar cells.

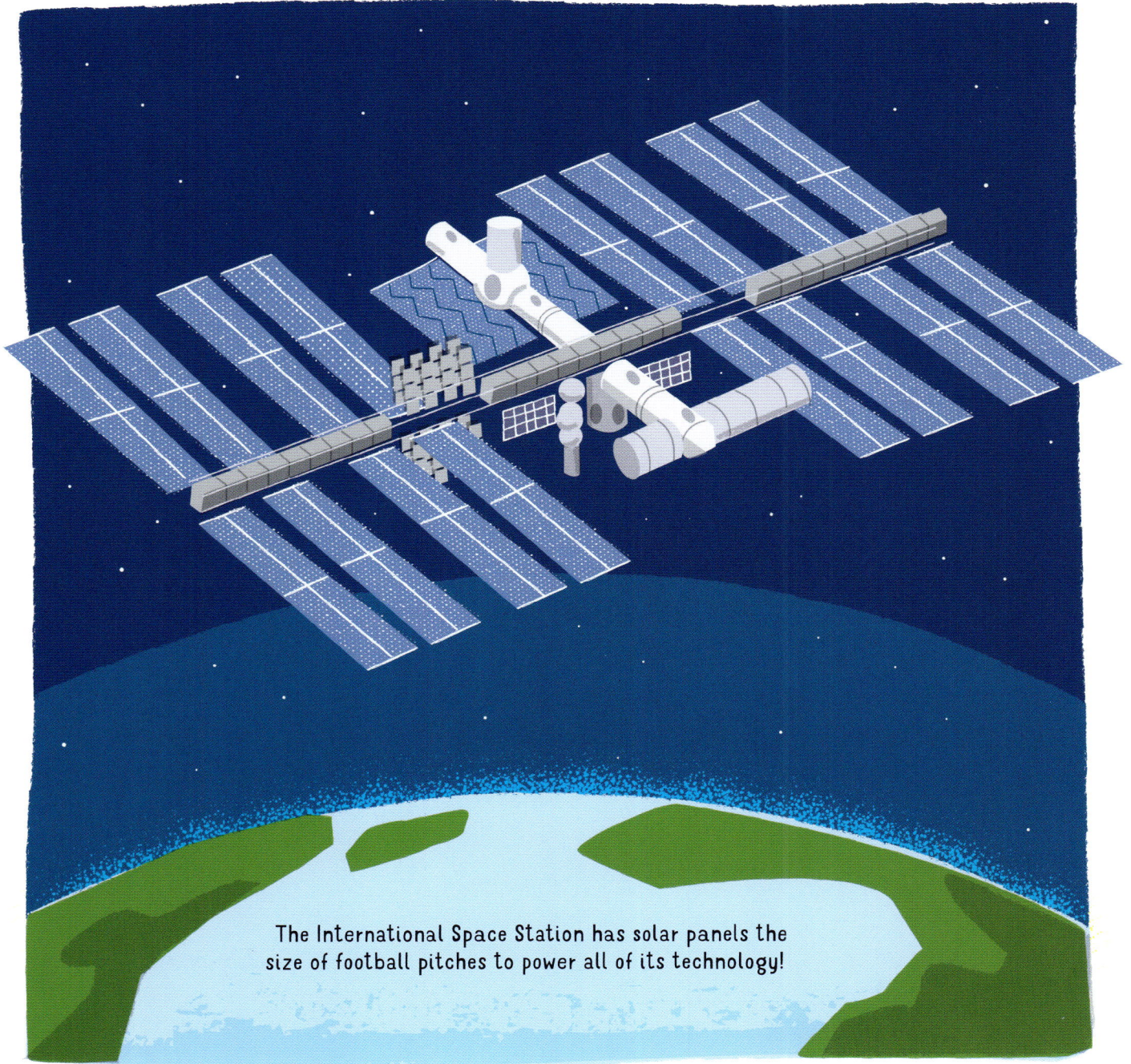

The International Space Station has solar panels the size of football pitches to power all of its technology!

SOLAR POWER STATIONS

Solar power stations, which are often called solar farms, consist of many solar PV panels or lots of mirrors linked together. A solar farm generates a lot of electricity from one site. A grid takes the electricity from the solar power station to businesses, homes and towns away from the site.

Solar farm size

A solar farm needs a large area of land for two reasons. First, there needs to be enough mirrors or panels to harvest a large amount of solar radiation. Secondly, the mirrors and panels need to be spaced out so they do not shade each other. Power companies often build solar farms on wasteland, dry scrubland or deserts.

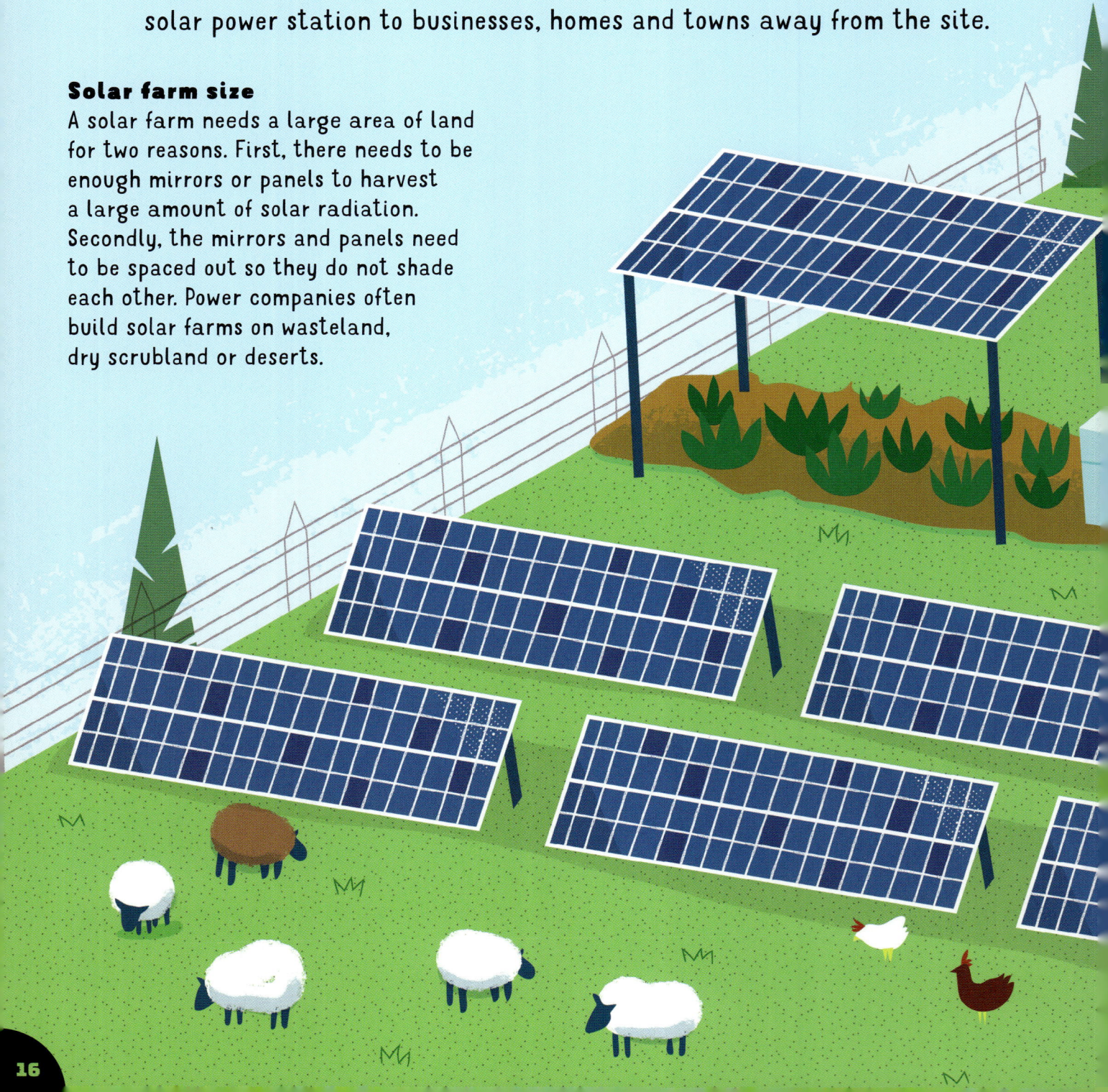

Building solar farms

Power companies usually bulldoze land to remove plants that might get in the way or shade mirrors or panels, and to make sure the ground is completely flat. Concentrated Solar Power (CSP) systems need level ground so that all of the mirrors can reflect lots of light whatever the position of the Sun. They are often built in a spot with a good water supply nearby, such as a river, to take water for making steam to turn the turbines.

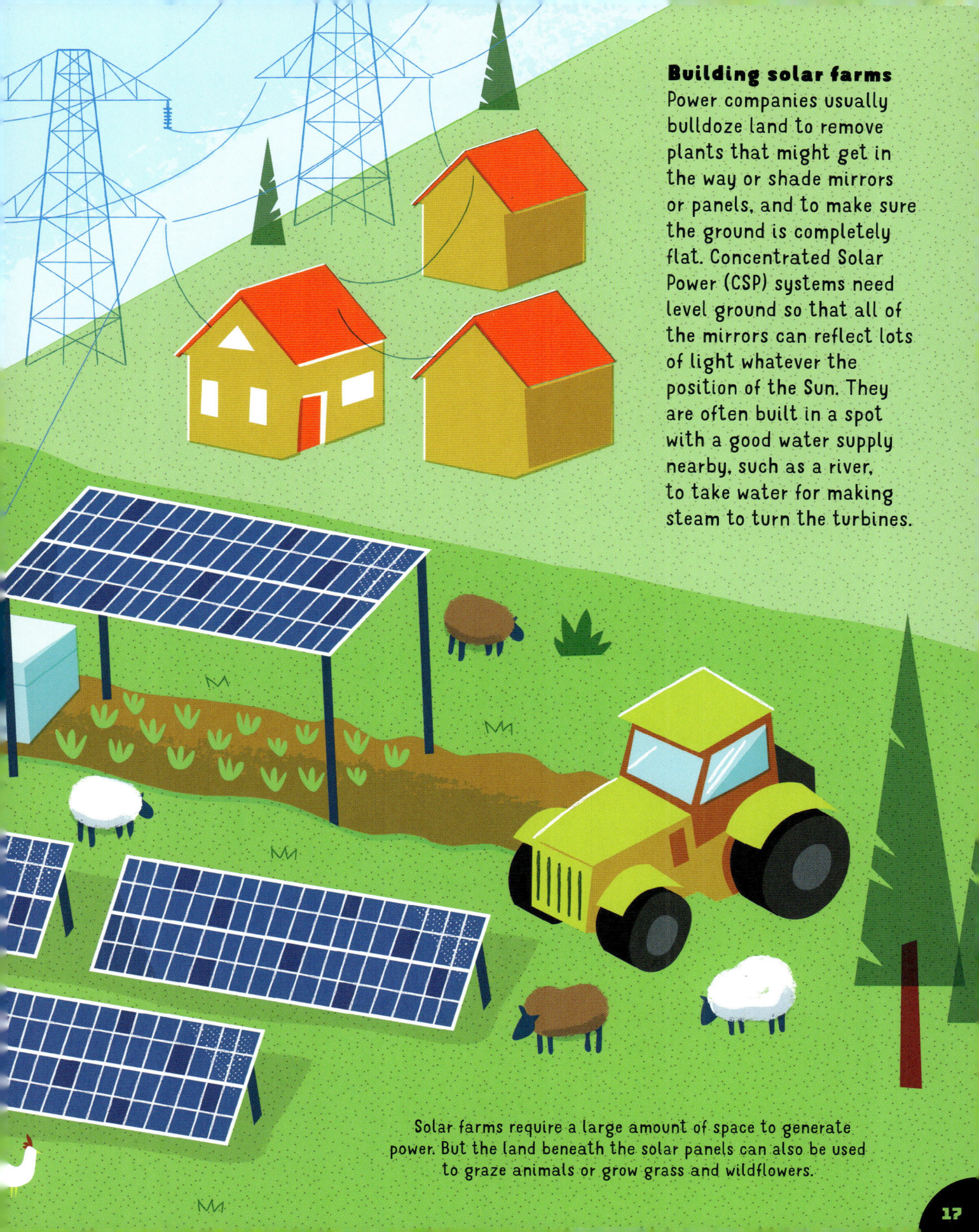

Solar farms require a large amount of space to generate power. But the land beneath the solar panels can also be used to graze animals or grow grass and wildflowers.

SOLAR POWER AND POLLUTION

When solar power stations are up and running, they do not produce any gases that are harmful to the atmosphere. However, making solar cells and building solar power stations can affect both the planet and living things.

Solar cell snags

Factories burn coal to heat sand and turn it into silicon for solar cells. Burning coal releases greenhouse gases into the atmosphere. Mining rocks to extract metals, such as the lead used in solar cells, produces holes and lots of waste rock. Rain can wash away remaining metals from the rock, polluting and poisoning rivers and lakes.

Substances used to make solar cells can be health hazards for people who make the cells.

Power station problems

Making the mirrors and the concrete needed to build CSP stations uses electricity. This mostly comes from fossil fuel power stations that release greenhouse gases. The lorries and other vehicles used to carry solar power parts and clear land for power stations burn diesel oil that also releases greenhouse gases.

Solar cell substances

Solar cells are made using small amounts of poisonous substances. Lead is used in the electrical parts of cells and panels and cadmium is sometimes used instead of silicon. These substances are not poisonous in small quantities. However, solar cell factory workers who deal with cadmium or lead over a long period of time could become sick.

Setting up solar power causes some problems, but it is still far less polluting than coal power.

HOW EFFICIENT IS SOLAR POWER?

Solar panel efficiency is a measure of how much sunlight a solar panel can convert into usable electricity.

Comparing efficiency

At present, most solar cells are made from silicon, which converts about one-fifth of the solar radiation reaching its surface into electricity. The other four-fifths is wasted. Some solar cells are made from different photovoltaic materials that waste only half of the energy they capture.

Solar power stations

Solar power stations convert about a third of the solar energy hitting their mirrors into electricity. This is as efficient as the conversion of coal into electricity in power stations. However, coal supplies are limited, whereas there is an endless supply of sunlight so wastage is not expensive.

Looking after solar farms

Solar cells and mirrors generate less power if they are shaded or dirty. Solar panels are made of lots of small cells connected together. If light is blocked from just a few cells, they can prevent the whole panel from working. Power company workers look after solar farms by cutting down trees and other plants that shade panels. They check that the motors which make the mirrors move and pump melted salt or oil through the pipes work properly. They may also clean the mirrors and cells.

A worker checks a mirror at a solar farm for any damage, dirt or other problems that might affect its efficiency.

THE COST OF SOLAR POWER

The major cost of solar power for electricity is building the power stations and making and installing solar panels. Once this is done, the costs for running and looking after a solar power station are low. That's because there is no fuel to buy as there would be for fossil fuel power generation.

Starting up stations

All power stations cost a lot to set up before they can start generating electricity. Power companies have to buy land and equipment, such as turbines. At first, solar power stations cost more to set up than fossil fuel power stations, partly because they use newer and more expensive technology. Improvements in technology mean many solar power stations cost less today. Also, once they are up and running solar power stations generate cheaper electricity than even the world's cheapest new coal plants.

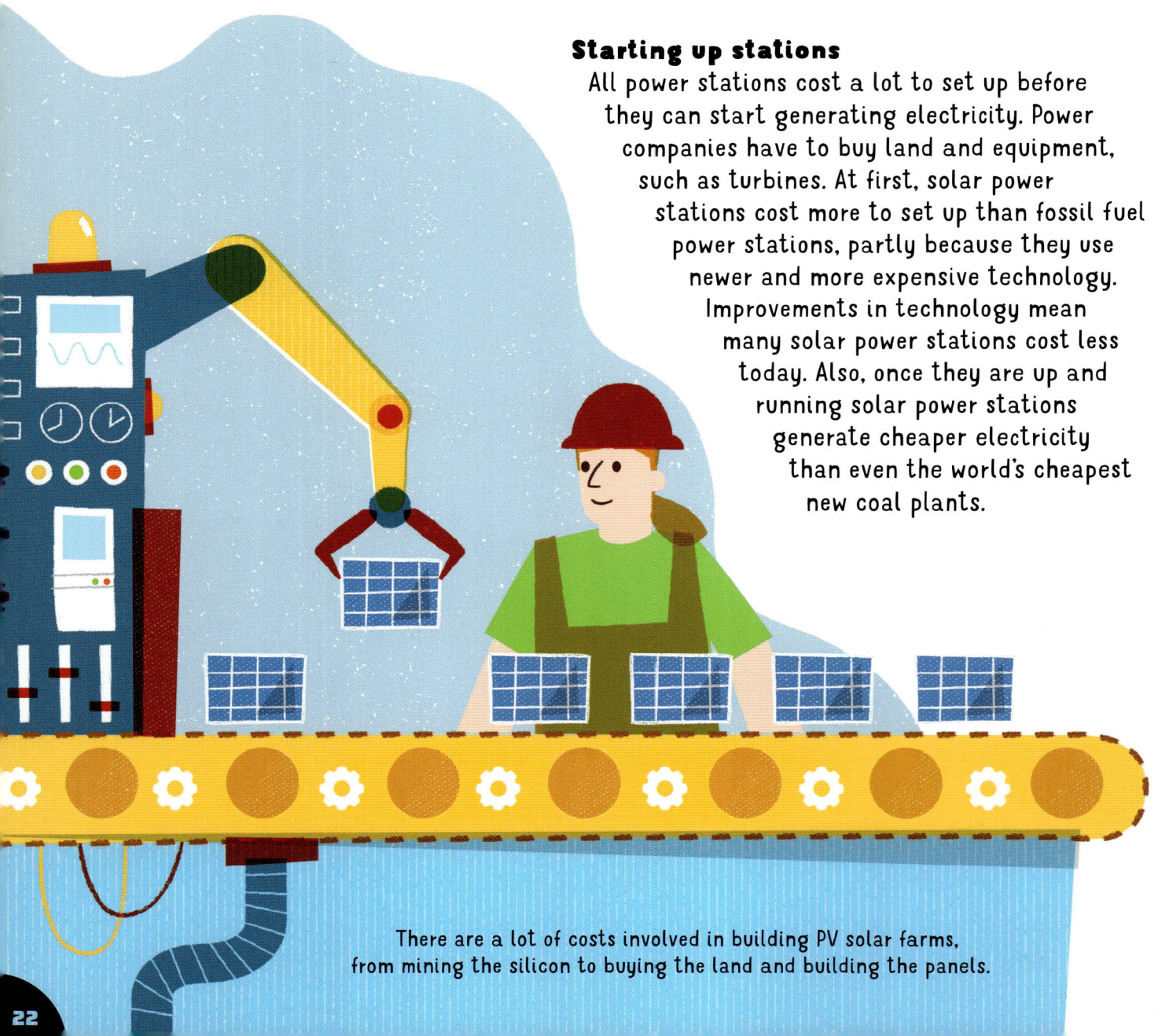

There are a lot of costs involved in building PV solar farms, from mining the silicon to buying the land and building the panels.

Solar panel prices

Silicon crystals used to make solar cells are expensive and PV solar farms require large areas of land. Both of these things make PV solar farms expensive to build. Although they are still not cheap, there has been a huge decrease in cost in recent years. In fact, solar farms can now be set up for over 80 per cent less than in 2010. As more solar farms are built, solar panel makers have been able to develop more cost-effective parts.

Solar power is getting cheaper all the time, as scientists invent new technologies to make it more efficient.

ENCOURAGING SOLAR POWER USE

In an attempt to tackle climate change, governments around the world have agreed targets to reduce greenhouse gases released by their countries. To help them achieve these targets, many governments are encouraging solar power industries.

Helping to set up solar power

One way governments do this is by subsidising new solar projects. They make payments or loans to help power companies and individuals pay for the costs of setting up solar power systems. Subsidies have been used before. Many governments have subsidised non-renewables such as fossil fuel power in the past.

Many countries subsidise solar projects in order to help develop a clean, renewable power supply.

Reducing fossil fuels

Governments also ask fossil fuel power companies to reduce the greenhouse gases they create. Power companies that previously relied only on fossil fuels have begun setting up solar farms or other renewable power stations to help them achieve this.

Buying excess solar electricity

Another way governments encourage solar power is to buy electricity that privately owned solar stations or panels generate. When companies and individuals make more electricity than they need from their solar power systems, they can feed the extra power into the grid to become mains electricity. By paying for this renewable electricity, governments encourage companies and individuals to generate more of it.

Climate protestors encourage governments to cut greenhouse gases by investing in renewable power, such as solar.

NEW SOLAR TECHNOLOGY

There are new solar power technologies being invented every year. Here are some of the new solar technologies that are being developed and used today.

Floating solar PV

'Floatovoltaics' are photovoltaic solar power systems mounted on a structure that floats on reservoirs, dams and other areas of water. Floating solar farms are cheaper to set up as they don't rely on buying land. Also, research suggests that floating solar panels produce up to 10 per cent more power than land-based systems due to the cooling effect of water. Land-based panels can overheat.

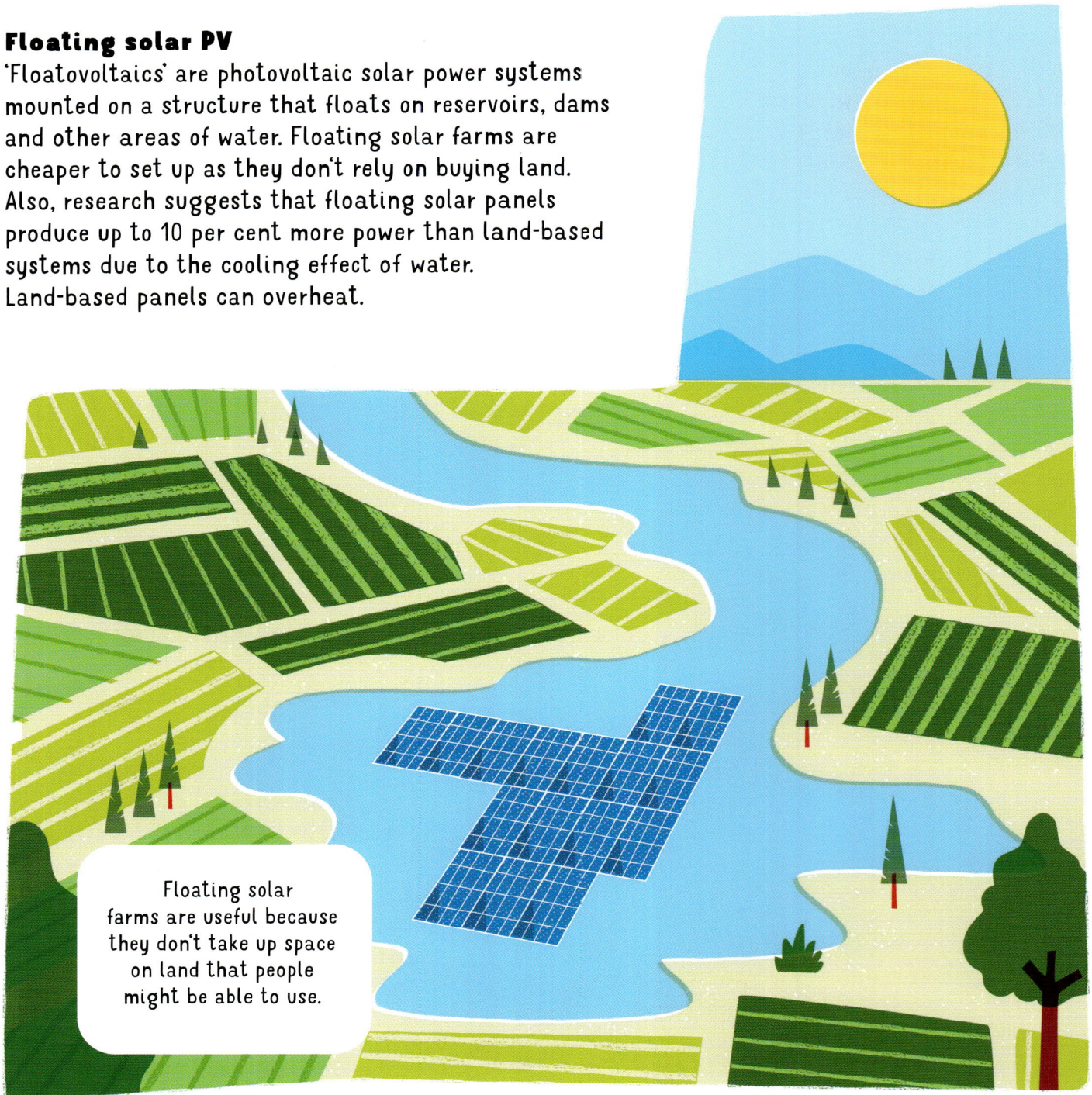

Floating solar farms are useful because they don't take up space on land that people might be able to use.

Invisible power

Some people think that solar panels on buildings or large areas of panels in fields are unsightly. New building-integrated photovoltaics are PV materials that are used to replace building materials in parts of a building. They can look like tiles on a roof or windows in a wall for example, so they can provide power without being so noticeable.

Solar panels

Building-integrated photovoltaics are roofs, tiles, windows or building cladding that generate electricity from the Sun.

Power you can wear?

In future, we could even wear solar cells! Researchers have been working on ways of making fabric with solar cells inside. Fabrics with flexible solar cells could be made into T-shirts, coats and other clothing to provide power for portable electronic devices, such as phones.

THE FUTURE OF SOLAR POWER

The future looks bright for solar power. Around the world, more and more countries are producing increasing amounts of energy from renewables instead of fossil fuels, with solar power playing a leading role.

Increasing availability

As more countries invest in solar power, solar technology will get cheaper and more people will be able to afford solar electricity. The use of better storage technology, such as battery storage units, is also helping increase their efficiency. One day, more efficient and adaptable solar panels may even be able to generate electricity to power more vehicles and cut the use of oil for fuel.

Looking ahead

Some regions of the world will expand their use of solar power faster than others. In some, such as North Africa, wind or running water are not so plentiful as sunshine, so solar power may be the only renewable energy resource available. In others, such as the USA, solar power will help reduce greenhouse gases and make the country less reliable on fuel from other countries.

Some experts believe that solar power could generate half of the world's electricity by 2050!

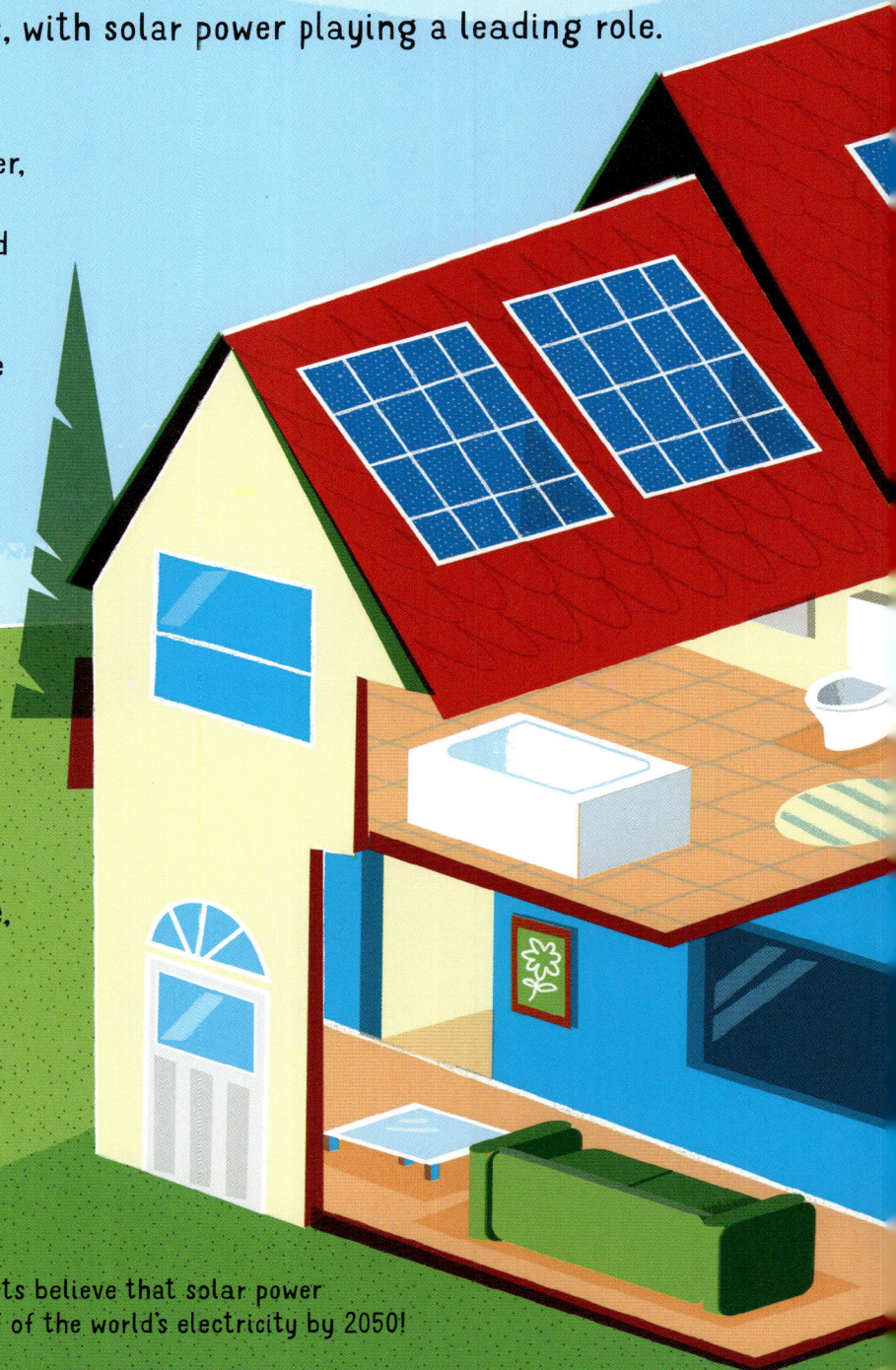

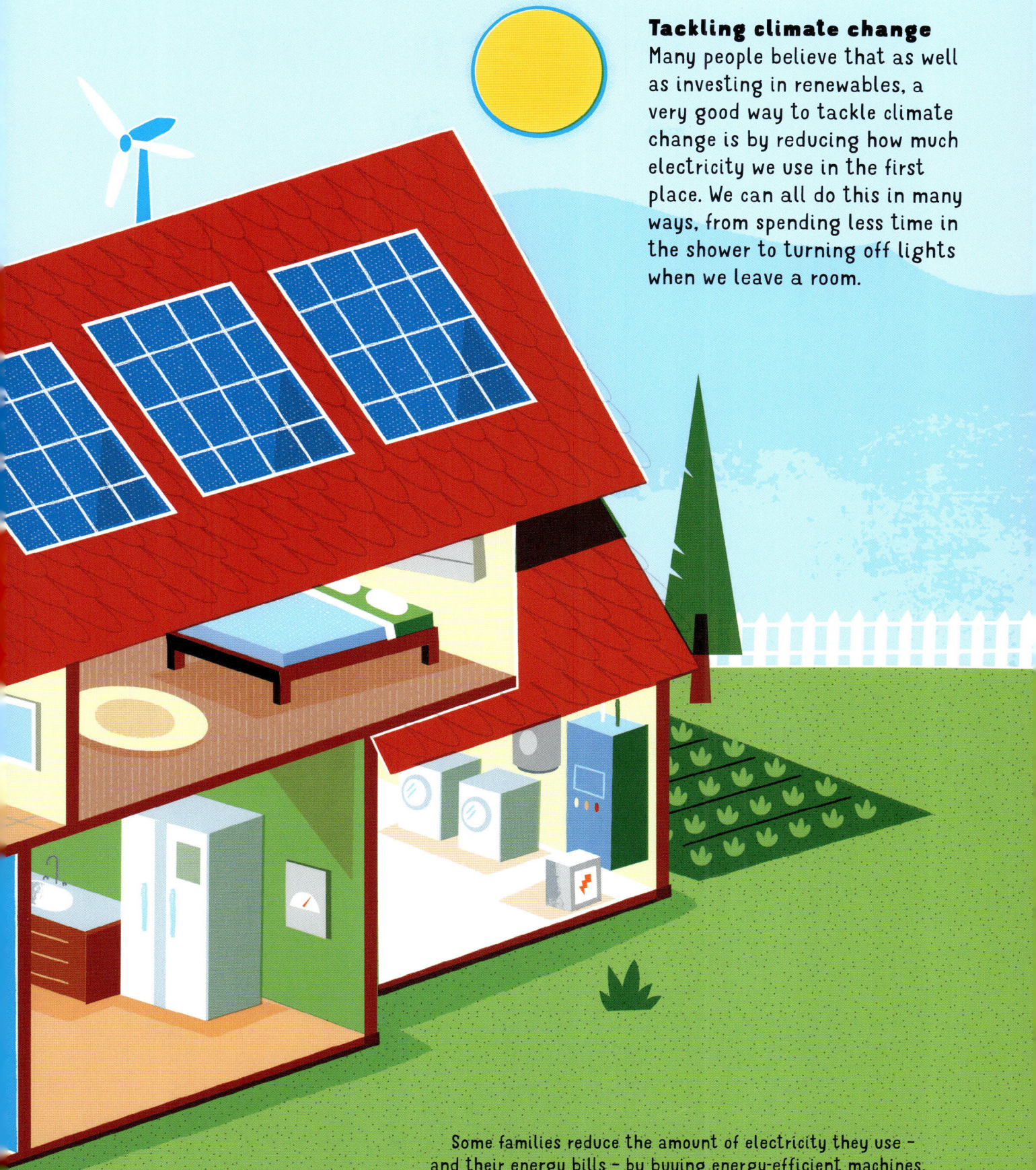

Tackling climate change

Many people believe that as well as investing in renewables, a very good way to tackle climate change is by reducing how much electricity we use in the first place. We can all do this in many ways, from spending less time in the shower to turning off lights when we leave a room.

Some families reduce the amount of electricity they use – and their energy bills – by buying energy-efficient machines, such as fridges and washing machines.

THINK FURTHER

Using solar power is a hot topic, with people often disagreeing about the pros and cons of using solar power to generate electricity. What do you think?

For and against

Solar cells and solar power stations do not work when the Sun isn't shining.
But ...
Fossil fuel power stations can work all the time, so long as they have enough fuel.

Burning fossil fuels creates large amounts of greenhouse gases that cause climate change.
But ...
Solar power stations do not release greenhouse gases when they are up and running.

Solar power saves money because unlike fossil fuel power it is not costing the world money due to the effects of climate change, such as crop failures.
But ...
Solar power is more expensive than other renewable energy sources.

Solar power farms require no fuels and are cheaper to run than fossil fuel power stations.
But ...
Solar power farms cost a lot to set up and take up a lot of land.

Which of these statements do you agree with? Why?
You could do some research or check back through the book
to help you decide what you think. Or talk about it with a friend.

GLOSSARY

atmosphere mix of gases surrounding the Earth up to the edge of space.

battery store of electrical energy.

carbon dioxide gas found in air that is produced by living things, or by burning fossil fuels.

conduct allow electricity to pass through. Copper in electric wires conducts well.

current flow of electricity.

efficiency when resources, such as energy, are made best use of and are not wasted.

fossil fuel fuel, such as coal, formed over millions of years from the remains of living things.

global warming increase in the average temperature of the Earth's atmosphere and oceans.

greenhouse gas gas, such as carbon dioxide, that stores heat in the atmosphere.

grid system of wires and pylons for sending electricity across a wide area.

habitat place where particular types of animals or plants normally live.

mains electricity electricity supplied through the grid to users from power stations.

microgenerating using your own equipment and the Sun, wind or water to produce all the heat and electricity that you need.

non-renewable energy resources, such as coal and oil, that are running out as they are not replaced when used.

photovoltaic describes the property of converting sunlight into electricity.

pollution harmful substances that make air, water or soil less safe to use or live in.

power station factory for generating electricity.

radiation energy that moves in narrow lines or rays.

renewable energy resources that are replaced naturally and can be used without running out.

solar cell device usually containing silicon that converts solar to electrical energy.

solar farm area with many solar thermal mirrors or solar panels to generate electricity.

solar panel structure containing solar cells linked together to increase electricity output.

solar receiver part of a solar thermal system that mirrors focus heat upon.

subsidise pay to support something and encourage its success.

turbine a type of machine through which liquid or gas flows and turns a special wheel with blades in order to produce power.

INDEX